Food Trucks

Julie Murray

Abdo Kids Junior
is an Imprint of Abdo Kids
abdobooks.com

Abdo
TRUCKS AT WORK
Kids

abdobooks.com

Published by Abdo Kids, a division of ABDO, P.O. Box 398166, Minneapolis, Minnesota 55439.
Copyright © 2024 by Abdo Consulting Group, Inc. International copyrights reserved in all countries.
No part of this book may be reproduced in any form without written permission from the publisher.
Abdo Kids Junior™ is a trademark and logo of Abdo Kids.

Printed in the United States of America, North Mankato, Minnesota.

052023

092023

THIS BOOK CONTAINS
RECYCLED MATERIALS

Photo Credits: Getty Images, Shutterstock

Production Contributors: Teddy Borth, Jennie Forsberg, Grace Hansen

Design Contributors: Candice Keimig, Pakou Moua

Library of Congress Control Number: 2022946715

Publisher's Cataloging-in-Publication Data

Names: Murray, Julie, author.

Title: Food trucks / by Julie Murray

Description: Minneapolis, Minnesota : Abdo Kids, 2024 | Series: Trucks at work | Includes online resources
    and index.

Identifiers: ISBN 9781098266141 (lib. bdg.) | ISBN 9781098266844 (ebook) | ISBN 9781098267193
    (Read-to-me ebook)

Subjects: LCSH: Trucks--Juvenile literature. | Vehicles--Juvenile literature. | Food trucks--Juvenile
    literature.

Classification: DDC 388.32--dc23

Table of Contents

Food Trucks

Food trucks **prepare**, cook, and sell food.

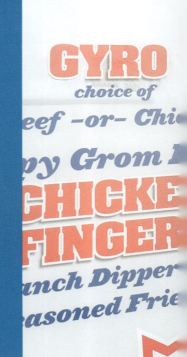

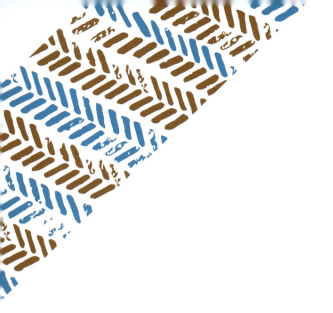

They are restaurants

on wheels!

The taco truck is here.

Marco gets extra salsa.

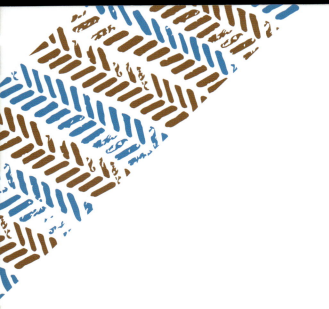

The **BBQ** truck is here.

Ribs are on the menu!

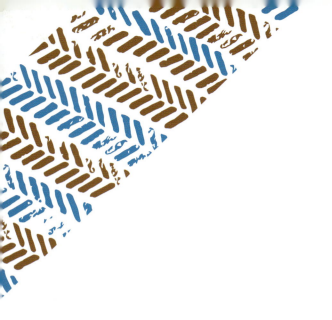

The pizza truck is here. It has a lot of good toppings.

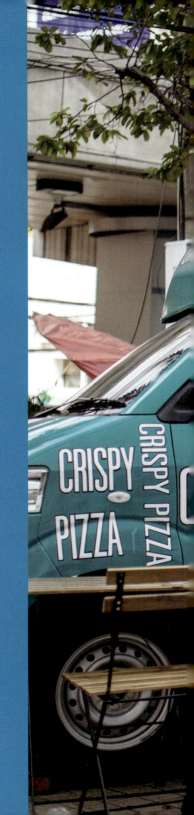

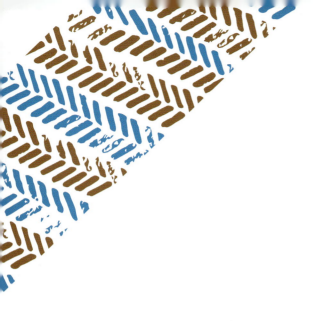

The burger truck is here.

Lon orders veggie burgers.

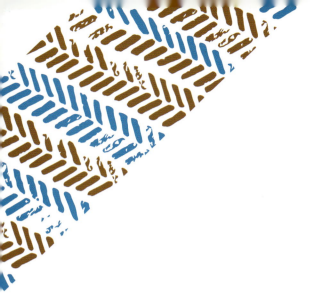

The donut truck is here.

The donuts are colorful!

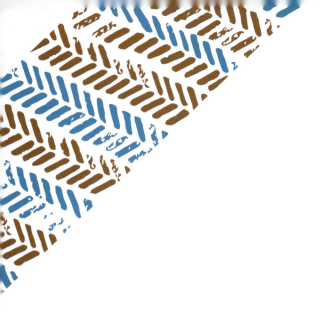

The ice cream truck is here.

It has fun flavors!

59 St - Columbus Ci

SUNDAES · SHAKES

FUN-TIME

FUN-TIME
MILKSHAKE

SMOOTHIE INC.
328 TEN-EYCK ST.
BK. N.Y. 11206

Have you eaten at a

food truck?

More Food Trucks

dessert truck

hot dog truck

pasta truck

sandwich truck

Glossary

BBQ
short for barbecue.

prepare
to make ready.

Index

Abdo Kids ONLINE
FREE! ONLINE MULTIMEDIA RESOURCES

Visit **abdokids.com** to access crafts, games, videos, and more!

Use Abdo Kids code

TFK6141

or scan this QR code!